CW01512514

Original title:

Embers of Joy

Copyright © 2025 Swan Charm

All rights reserved.

Author: Olivia Oja

ISBN HARDBACK: 978-1-80560-263-7

ISBN PAPERBACK: 978-1-80560-728-1

Flashes of Heart's Embrace

In the quiet night, stars stir,
A gentle whisper, love's soft purr.
Moments linger, time stands still,
In the glow, our hearts do fill.

Holding hands beneath the moon,
Each heartbeat sings a timeless tune.
Eyes entwined, a soulful dance,
Lost in dreams, another chance.

Memories created in soft light,
Flickers of warmth, pure delight.
Every glance, a secret shared,
In the silence, we are bared.

With every beat, our spirits rise,
A tender bond that never lies.
Through the shadows, we find grace,
In the flashes of heart's embrace.

A tapestry of moments spun,
Unified, we are but one.
In the twilight, shadows blend,
Love's sweet echo, never end.

Warm Reflections on Twilight's Edge

Glistening rays as daylight fades,
Softly skimming through the glades.
Golden hues wrap the trees,
Nature hums a gentle breeze.

Whispers of dusk embrace the land,
With every step, we take a stand.
Echoes dance in fading light,
Promising dreams amid the night.

Silhouettes in a soft hue,
Moments shared, just me and you.
Together we find, as shadows blend,
A fleeting warmth that won't rescind.

In the calm, our souls conspire,
To ignite our hearts' desire.
As stars ignite in velvet skies,
Warm reflections spark our ties.

Holding tight, the twilight lingers,
In the air, a warm feeling fingers.
With each breath, the night unfolds,
As the story of love retolds.

Embrace of the Glimmering

Underneath the starlit skies,
Glimmers spark as daylight dies.
In the hush, our spirits twine,
Under stars, our hearts align.

Every flicker a promise bright,
Guiding us through the velvet night.
In this moment, we are whole,
Embrace of glimmering, body and soul.

Faint whispers of dreams once near,
Feelings blossom, crystal clear.
As shadows dance upon the ground,
In this magic, love is found.

Holding on as stars collide,
Together here, we must confide.
With every sparkle, everything fades,
Inside the glimmer, our love cascades.

In the end, as dawn will break,
Softly, we will not forsake.
For in the universe's vast seams,
Lives the beauty of our dreams.

Ashes of Laughter

In shadows of mirth, echoes remain,
Flickers of joy, a bittersweet pain.
Memories linger, like whispers in time,
Ashes of laughter, once bright, now sublime.

Through tears of the past, we find our way,
In remnants of giggles, the heart learns to play.
A dance in the darkness, a flicker of light,
Ashes of laughter, a warm, sweet delight.

Sparks of Bliss

In the quiet of dawn, soft ripples arise,
Sparks of bliss dance under brightening skies.
Hope flickers gently, in the hush of the morn,
A promise of joy, with each day reborn.

Moments of kindness, woven with thread,
Sparks of connection through words that we've said.
Radiance flows freely, with love intertwined,
Sparks of bliss shimmering, hearts gently aligned.

Tinders of Happiness

Nestled within, where feelings ignite,
Tinders of happiness flicker so bright.
In silence they smolder, waiting to rise,
Glimmers of laughter, a warm, soft surprise.

Each moment a treasure, a heartbeat, a glow,
Tinders of happiness radiate slow.
In dance with the shadows, they flourish and bloom,
Kindling the fire that banishes gloom.

Glows of Serenity

Under starlit skies, the world holds its breath,
Glows of serenity banish all regret.
Whispers of calm brush against weary skin,
A moment of peace, where stillness begins.

Through valleys of silence, we wander and roam,
Glows of serenity create a sweet home.
In each gentle breeze, a promise unfolds,
Wrapped in the warmth of stories untold.

Kaleidoscope of Cheer

Colors dance in the day,
Laughter ringing so clear,
Joyful hearts on display,
A kaleidoscope of cheer.

Sunshine spills like sweet dreams,
Painting smiles in the air,
Every moment redeems,
Wrapped in love and care.

Whispers of hope unfurl,
In gardens where we play,
The magic starts to swirl,
Chasing shadows away.

Waves of giggles cascade,
Through fields of golden light,
Memories softly laid,
In the warmth of the night.

Together we create,
A tapestry so bright,
In friendship, we await,
New dawns that feel right.

Enchantment in the Ashes

From embers, dreams arise,
Whispers of times gone past,
Beauty through tears and sighs,
Enchantment found at last.

In twilight's gentle glow,
Stories linger and sway,
Flickering soft and slow,
A dance of night and day.

The past, a sacred tale,
Etched in shadows and light,
Healing hearts that prevail,
With warmth through every night.

Ashes cradle the night,
Nurtured by love's embrace,
In silence, there's delight,
As we reclaim our space.

Hope springs from what has been,
Resilience in our veins,
In the ashes, we glean,
Life's lessons through the pains.

Luminous Memories

Moments bright as the sun,
Captured in heart's deep reel,
Every laugh, every run,
Luminous memories feel.

Echoes of voices near,
Softly whisper our name,
In the twilight, we hear,
The joy within the frame.

Stars twinkle overhead,
Guiding us through the night,
With every tear we've shed,
We achieve the pure light.

Painting dreams with our thoughts,
The canvas of our days,
In the battles we've fought,
We've found so many ways.

Carried through endless time,
The laughter and the pain,
In perfect rhythm, rhyme,
Life's tapestry remains.

Twilight's Embrace

As sun dips low in skies,
The world begins to sigh,
Wrap me in twilight's ties,
As stars start to comply.

Colors blur into dreams,
The horizon melts gold,
In shadows, magic gleams,
Whispers softly unfold.

Each heartbeat syncs with light,
Nature's gentle caress,
Through the silk of the night,
We find a world, no less.

Emotions intertwine,
In the dimming glow's grace,
Life's moments, they align,
In twilight's warm embrace.

Here, dreams gently flow,
With every breath we take,
In this peace, we will grow,
As night begins to wake.

Twilight's Embrace

The sun dips low, a gentle sigh,
Stars emerge, the night draws nigh.
Colors blend in soft retreat,
Whispers of dusk, so bittersweet.

Shadows stretch, the world anew,
Moonlit paths, a silver hue.
Taking steps with tender grace,
In the quiet, we find our place.

Time stands still, a fleeting glance,
Underneath the night's romance.
Hearts awaken, dreams take flight,
In the warmth of fading light.

Each moment dances in the dark,
Echoing the last day's spark.
Holding close what's ours to save,
In twilight's arms, we gently wave.

Flickering Heartstrings

Melodies drift upon the air,
Notes entwined without a care.
A gentle strum, a whispered tone,
In this music, we are home.

Rhythms pulse within our chests,
Creating warmth through fleeting quests.
Dancing lights, they flicker bright,
Binding souls in sheer delight.

Harmony wraps us in a dream,
Sailing softly down the stream.
Every beat, a love so true,
Sounding out our hearts' debut.

In the silence, secrets lie,
A serenade beneath the sky.
Through notes and chords, we'll always find,
The music of our hearts entwined.

White-hot Wonder

In the stillness, sparks ignite,
Nature glows with purest light.
Every breath a blaze of fire,
Awakens deep, our wild desire.

Snowflakes dance like dreams in flight,
Blanketing the world in white.
Whispers crawl through frosty air,
Instill a warmth beyond compare.

Eyes alight with pure delight,
Chasing shadows, chasing light.
Magic twirls both near and far,
Illuminating who we are.

In the glow, our spirits rise,
Beneath the vast, embracing skies.
A feeling born from purest wonder,
A love that pulls us from down under.

Sizzle of Delight

From the pan, aromas rise,
Savory treats beneath the skies.
Each bite, a dance of spice and zest,
On the tongue, a searching quest.

Crispy edges, tender core,
With every taste, we crave for more.
Flavors burst, a sweet acclaim,
In this kitchen, we find fame.

Sizzle, pop, the food's alive,
New creations in which we thrive.
Gather 'round, our laughter blends,
In shared meals, our love transcends.

In the heat, joy intertwines,
With every dish, our heart aligns.
At this table where dreams unite,
We savor life, our pure delight.

Searing Laughter

In shadows deep, we find our spark,
A jolt of joy, igniting the dark.
Echoes of joy, a wild delight,
That dances and spins in the heart of night.

With every chuckle that fills the air,
We weave our tales, our laughter to share.
A symphony born from moments bright,
Binding our souls in the softest light.

In fleeting whispers, we chase the fun,
A golden thread, we've just begun.
Through bursts of glee, we come alive,
In searing laughter, we truly thrive.

Oh, life unfolds in riotous play,
With every giggle, we drift away.
We grasp the joy, let worries fade,
In the warmth of laughter, dreams are made.

Hold tight to this, our timeless song,
For in such moments, we all belong.
Let laughter be the light we seek,
In searing laughter, we're never weak.

Dreaming in Warm Tones

Beneath the sky, where colors blend,
We drift on dreams, where spirits mend.
In shades of gold, in hues of red,
Whispers of hopes that gently spread.

Softly we wander through twilight's grace,
Each touch of warmth, a soft embrace.
In amber light, our fears subside,
We dance on clouds, our hearts our guide.

Through rose-tinted glasses, we see anew,
A world transformed, each shade so true.
In every heartbeat, a canvas bright,
Dreaming in warmth, till the close of night.

Embracing dusk, we let go the past,
In twilight's glow, our shadows cast.
With every breath, a new desire,
Igniting sparks, setting dreams on fire.

As stars emerge in the deepening blue,
We find our dreams in the light's soft hue.
With open hearts, we journey on,
In warm-toned dreams, we are reborn.

Solace in Light

When shadows loom and doubts arise,
We seek the brilliance in azure skies.
In every sunrise, a brand new chance,
To find our courage, our hearts to dance.

The gentle glow of a fading day,
Whispers of warmth to guide our way.
In golden beams, our worries cease,
Finding solace, embracing peace.

As twilight drapes its velvet cloak,
We gather strength in the words we spoke.
Each flicker bright tells tales of grace,
Illuminating hope in every space.

With open eyes, we face the night,
In the still of dusk, we find our light.
In silver beams that softly gleam,
We weave our dreams from threads of cream.

Wrapped in comfort, our spirits soar,
In solace found, we're afraid no more.
Let the light guide us, forever bright,
Together we stand, embracing the night.

Glowing Reminiscence

In quiet corners of the mind,
Old memories linger, sweetly intertwined.
Soft echoes dance in the amber hue,
Whispers of moments, both old and new.

Each faded photograph, a portal wide,
To places and faces where love resides.
In the glow of laughter, we find our way,
To relive the magic of yesterday.

A fragrance escapes, a wisp of time,
Carried on breezes, a gentle rhyme.
In glowing reminiscence, we hold so dear,
Echoes of joy, drawing ever near.

With every heartbeat, a story unfolds,
In the warmth of memories, our heart enfolds.
A tapestry woven with threads of gold,
In glowing whispers, our lives retold.

So let us cherish those moments bright,
In the glow of the past, our guiding light.
For in each reminiscence, we find our peace,
A gentle reminder that love won't cease.

Hearts Aglow

In the quiet of night, dreams take flight,
Whispers of love softly ignite.
Stars above twinkle bright,
As hearts aglow bask in light.

Every glance a cherished spark,
In shadows, we leave our mark.
With every heartbeat, we embark,
Together, we conquer the dark.

Gentle breezes carry our sighs,
Under the moon's watchful eyes.
Moments wrapped in sweet reprise,
In love's embrace, true joy lies.

With laughter that fills the air,
Every sorrow we learn to bear.
Together, we form a pair,
In our haven, free from care.

As dawn breaks, colors bloom,
Every heartbeat dispels the gloom.
In this garden, love will loom,
Hearts aglow, forever in tune.

Comfort in the Flicker

In the darkness, a flicker shines,
A beacon of warmth, love entwines.
Gentle glow of hope aligns,
With each heartbeat, sweet designs.

Soft shadows dance upon the wall,
A quiet whisper, an inviting call.
In the flicker, we rise and fall,
Comfort found in the small.

Hands held tight in shared embrace,
Creating a safe, sacred space.
In every flicker, we find grace,
In tender moments, we retrace.

Time stands still when hearts conspire,
With every flicker, we build our fire.
In every laugh, in joys, we tire,
A love that lifts, and never tires.

As night falls, let dreams ignite,
In the flicker, our futures bright.
Together, we chase the light,
Finding comfort in each night.

Serenity in Flickers

Flickering candles, a soft glow,
In tranquil spaces, moments flow.
Hearts find peace, and gentle knowing,
In the quiet, love is growing.

Each soft light a tale to tell,
In hushed tones, we weave our spell.
In flickers bright, we find our shell,
A sanctuary where we dwell.

Whispers of dreams in evening air,
In every flicker, we find care.
With each sigh, we're almost there,
Where silence blooms, hearts bare.

As stillness wraps the world around,
In calm, our souls are tightly bound.
In flickers soft, we have found,
The solace in love profound.

When shadows fade at break of dawn,
In flickers, new hopes are drawn.
With every breath, a love reborn,
In serenity, we feel we're sworn.

Celestial Illuminations

Stars above in the night sky,
Celestial wonders, oh so high.
Each twinkle a secret sigh,
Illuminations that never die.

In the stillness, we gaze in awe,
Nature's beauty, pure and raw.
In heavenly light, we draw
Inspiration, a sacred law.

Galaxy whispers paint our dreams,
In cosmic flows, moonlight beams.
In the night, our spirit schemes,
With each star, our heart redeems.

Beneath the sky's vast tapestry,
We find our place, a mystery.
In every glow, there's unity,
A dance of love, a symphony.

As dawn approaches, shadows yaw,
The sun unfolds with a golden draw.
In celestial light, we stand in awe,
Eternal love, our heart's law.

Stories of Sun-kissed Days

In golden fields where laughter plays,
Children dance through sun-kissed days.
Breezes whisper tales of cheer,
Memories linger, always near.

Moments wrapped in warmth and light,
Every heart feels pure delight.
Nature sings with vibrant hues,
Painting skies in brilliant views.

The sun dips low, a gentle sigh,
As evening paints the sky on high.
Soft shadows stretch, the day departs,
But sun-kissed tales fill all our hearts.

Hidden Rays of Sunshine

In quiet glades where shadows fall,
Hidden rays heed nature's call.
They shimmer soft on emerald leaves,
Nurturing life, as the heart believes.

A gentle beam on a tired face,
Brings warmth and joy, a sweet embrace.
These fleeting glints, so full of grace,
Revive the soul's most cherished space.

Through cracks in stone, they break the gloom,
Beneath the weight of winter's bloom.
A promise shines, a truth to find,
In hidden rays, love intertwines.

Twilight's Tender Touch

As daylight wanes and colors blend,
Twilight whispers, a gentle friend.
Stars awaken, the moon's soft glow,
Invites the night with a tranquil flow.

Silhouettes dance on the horizon,
Nature sighs as day is done.
Birds settle down in nests so tight,
Embracing peace in the hush of night.

The world relaxes; time stands still,
As twilight wraps us with its will.
In every heartbeat, stillness flows,
A tender touch that softly glows.

The Glow of Yesterday

In the attic, memories reside,
A box of dreams we still confide.
Photos faded, smiles held dear,
Each glance recalls a bygone year.

The laughter spills from worn-out pages,
Stories told through all the stages.
Flickering lights of moments passed,
Enduring warmth from shadows cast.

Though time may fade, the glow remains,
A testament of love's sweet gains.
In every treasure lies a thread,
Connecting hearts to what we've said.

Flickering Joy

In shadows, laughter skips,
Bright as stars on velvet nights,
A dance of fleeting moments,
Echoes soft, like whispered lights.

Here, in smiles, we roam free,
Hearts like lanterns, gently sway,
With every tick, a heartbeat,
Flickering joy, here to stay.

Through the rain, a rainbow shows,
Promises in colors bright,
Each drop sings, a sweet repose,
Crafting dreams in sheer delight.

We chase the dawn's golden rays,
Embers flicker as we play,
In the warmth of shared embrace,
Finding joy in every way.

As the sweetest songs unwind,
In the hush of twilight's glow,
Together, love intertwined,
Celebrate the flickering flow.

Glimpse of the Divine

In moments quiet and still,
Nature whispers secrets clear,
A breeze carries ancient tales,
Inviting souls to come near.

Beneath the vast, starlit sky,
The cosmos hums a soft tune,
In every twinkle, a prayer,
Hearts aligned with the moon.

Each sunrise paints a new hope,
Colors bleed into the day,
In the silence, truths arise,
Guiding us along the way.

With every step on this path,
Faith and wonder intertwine,
A soft light breaks through the dark,
In each breath a glimpse divine.

In this world, we find our way,
Through the shadows and the shine,
Every heartbeat shouts the truth,
We are part of the divine.

Kindling Hope

In the quiet of the night,
Stars alight the darkened dome,
With each twinkle, dreams take flight,
Whispers bring the heart back home.

Shadows dance upon the wall,
Memories linger, warm and bright,
In the twilight, we recall,
The promise of dawn's soft light.

From the ashes, embers glow,
Courage finds its rise and place,
In the depths, seeds of grace sow,
Hope ignites, a gentle face.

Through the storms we learn to stand,
Hand in hand, we light the way,
With each step, a brighter land,
Kindling hope, come what may.

As the sun begins to rise,
Colors flood the waking earth,
In the stillness, we realize,
Every day brings new rebirth.

Warmth of Memories

In laughter shared, the echoes stay,
Time embraces every past,
Moments held in tender sway,
Through the veil, our shadows cast.

Soft whispers of the day gone by,
Rustle like leaves in the breeze,
In the heart, they gently lie,
Bringing comfort, sweet as ease.

Photographs in faded frames,
Capture smiles, each story told,
Each memory, like flickering flames,
A tapestry of love and gold.

Through the seasons, we will roam,
With the warmth of what we know,
Together finding our way home,
In the hearts of those we grow.

As dusk falls, we close our eyes,
Let the memories softly weave,
In the silence, love never dies,
In the warmth, forever believe.

Twilight's Bounty

In the hush of fading light,
Shadows dance with grace,
Stars peer through velvet night,
Whispers of dreams embrace.

Golden hues of day now gleam,
Softly fading into blue,
Nature's sigh, a soothing theme,
Twilight's bounty, pure and true.

Fields aglow with dusky gold,
Echoes of the sun's last kiss,
Stories of the night retold,
In this moment, find your bliss.

Gentle winds begin to blow,
Carrying the scent of pine,
With each breath, let wonders grow,
In the dusk, your heart align.

As day surrenders to the night,
Embrace the peace that lingers,
In twilight's soft and radiant light,
Hold the dreams within your fingers.

Flare of Glee

In the dance of joy we spin,
Laughter blooms like summer's rose,
Every heartbeat draws us in,
In the moment, glee bestows.

Sunrise paints the world anew,
With colors bright, the skies ignite,
Hope and wonder shining through,
In our hearts, pure delight.

Flickering like fireflies' glow,
Memories made in fleeting flight,
We chase the dreams that overflow,
In the warmth of shared delight.

Through the trials, we still rise,
Hand in hand, we'll face the climb,
Seeing magic in the skies,
Creating moments, lost in time.

Let the laughter fill the days,
With every step, let spirits soar,
In this life, we find our ways,
Together, seeking evermore.

Hearth of Gratitude

Gathered 'round the fire's glow,
Hearts are warm, the edges smooth,
With each story, love will flow,
In this place, we find our groove.

The crackling flames, a gentle sound,
Memories shared, a rich embrace,
In this haven, peace is found,
With every smile, we find our space.

Kindred spirits, woven tight,
Through laughter, sorrow, and the years,
In the hearth, we see the light,
With gratitude, we share our tears.

Each moment shared, a treasure bright,
Reminds us of the bonds we weave,
In every heart, a spark ignites,
In love's warmth, we truly believe.

The world outside may restless be,
Yet here, there's solace, pure and true,
In this hearth, our spirits free,
Together, always, me and you.

Auras of Radiance

Beneath the sky, where colors blend,
A tapestry of hues unfold,
Each moment shared, a joy to send,
In whispers of the stories told.

The sun dips low, with golden rays,
Casting spells of light and cheer,
In every heart, a glow that stays,
Filling our souls, warmth appears.

Across the fields, the fireflies gleam,
Illuminating paths unseen,
In the quiet, we dare to dream,
Aqueous visions of the serene.

With every heartbeat, colors swirl,
Radiance echoes through the air,
In harmony, as life unfurls,
A celestial dance, beyond compare.

In the night, the stars ignite,
Each a beacon shining bright,
With love as our guiding light,
We journey on, hearts taking flight.

Smoldering Smiles

In twilight's glow, secrets hide,
Soft laughter like a whispering tide.
Each glance ignites a fleeting fire,
Leaves us longing, hearts desire.

The warmth escapes from tender grins,
Wrapped in the moments where love begins.
A spark that dances, flickers bright,
Binding souls in the quiet night.

Through fragile dreams, we weave our fate,
Where every glance feels like a date.
In smoldering smiles, hearts connect,
A love profound, we can't neglect.

With every heartbeat, shadows play,
Creating worlds where we can stay.
These smoldering smiles, a sacred dance,
In each other's eyes, a fleeting chance.

Brighter in the Twilight

In the dusk, the world transforms,
Whispers caught in evening's charms.
Colors blend, a vibrant sight,
Everything feels so very right.

Hold my hand in this fleeting glow,
Together, we'll let our spirits flow.
Every star beginning to gleam,
Lighting our way through this sweet dream.

Brighter hearts against the night,
Softly shining, love's pure light.
In twilight's embrace, we'll make our way,
Finding joy in the end of day.

With each moment that we share,
Magic lingers in the air.
In the dusk, our shadows blend,
As love writes stories without end.

Dances in the Shadows

Beneath the moon's soft silver light,
We twirl and sway into the night.
With silent steps and hearts in tune,
The world fades beneath the moon.

In shadows deep, our laughter rings,
A melody the darkness brings.
Together lost, we take our flight,
In this dance, all feels just right.

Every twirl ignites the space,
A secret world, our special place.
Dancing close, we lose the bounds,
In whispered dreams, our love resounds.

These flights of fancy, wild and free,
In twilight's hold, just you and me.
We sway and spin where shadows fall,
In this sweet moment, we have it all.

Warmth Beneath the Ashes

In ember's glow, a story waits,
Love ignites through time's vast gates.
With every scar, a tale unfurls,
A warmth beneath the ashes curls.

Memories flicker, soft and bright,
Carried forth on wings of night.
Within the silence, hearts will share,
The treasures hidden everywhere.

A gentle touch, a soothing balm,
In this chaos, we find calm.
Through trials faced, the flame survives,
Kindled love that forever thrives.

Beyond the flames that once had roared,
A bond is forged, a love restored.
In the quiet, hear the call,
Warmth beneath the ashes, we stand tall.

Flames of Contentment

In the quiet of the night,
A flicker, glowing bright,
Whispers soft on the breeze,
Setting every doubt at ease.

Moments wrapped in gentle light,
A heart that feels so right,
Embers dance in still air,
Filling souls with love and care.

Dreams woven in the flame,
No two are quite the same,
Each spark a wish set free,
Crafting joy and harmony.

In shadows, warmth does dwell,
A story only time can tell,
Where laughter meets the spark,
Guiding us through every dark.

Hold the fire, let it grow,
In its warmth, let kindness flow,
Together we will find our way,
In this heart, forever stay.

Shimmers of Positivity

In the dawn's first embrace,
Golden light fills the space,
Hope dances on the ground,
With every heartbeat, it's found.

Colors burst with pure delight,
Chasing away the night,
Each moment gleams and shines,
Life unfolds in grand designs.

Look around, see the glow,
In the smiles, let it grow,
A world painted with cheer,
Radiant, warm, and clear.

Every step a brand new start,
Igniting the open heart,
With laughter as our song,
Together, we all belong.

Hold the spark, let it rise,
Reflecting in joyful eyes,
In the shimmers, find the way,
To brighter, happier days.

Breaths of Warmth

In the gentle autumn air,
Whispers of love everywhere,
A blanket soft with embrace,
Filling hearts with tender grace.

Each sigh a soothing sound,
In harmony, we are bound,
The world wraps in its glow,
As the seeds of kindness grow.

Sunsets drape the evening sky,
Fireside tales that never die,
Cocooned in warmth so sweet,
Every moment feels complete.

Through the chill, we move near,
Sharing joys, shedding fear,
With each breath, feel the peace,
In this warmth, our hearts release.

Together, in this space,
Finding our rightful place,
Breaths of warmth, soft and clear,
A symphony for all to hear.

Rays of Cheer

Morning breaks, the sun awakes,
Painting gold on silver lakes,
Each ray a promise so bright,
Chasing shadows, bringing light.

Laughter dances in the breeze,
Stirring leaves on friendly trees,
A melody in the air,
In this moment, we all care.

Every glance, a spark of joy,
Finding peace in every ploy,
With friends, our hearts take flight,
Boundless love, a pure delight.

Through the storms, we'll persevere,
Guided always by our cheer,
With every step, we're strong,
Together is where we belong.

So let the rays shine through,
In every heart, a vibrant hue,
With joy and hope we blend,
In the light, together, we mend.

Tapestry of Radiant Moments

Threads of gold in twilight weave,
Memories dance, as hearts believe.
Each smile a stitch, in time they mend,
A tapestry bright, where dreams ascend.

Whispers of joy on gentle breeze,
Moments like petals, falling with ease.
Soft laughter echoes, sweet and light,
A canvas alive, in colors bright.

Sunset kisses the world anew,
Each glimmering star, a wish in view.
Weaving our stories, hand in hand,
In this radiant land, together we stand.

Time weaves its tale, both tender and bold,
In the fabric of life, memories unfold.
Through laughter and tears, the stitches align,
Creating a masterpiece, yours and mine.

Light in the Dusk

A glow beckons as day meets night,
Whispers of peace in the fading light.
Shadows dance on the horizon's edge,
Where dreams awaken, the heart will pledge.

Stars blink softly, a celestial play,
Guiding lost souls on their wandering way.
The moon, a guardian, watches us near,
In dusky embraces, we banish our fear.

Moments freeze in twilight's grace,
Every heartbeat finds its place.
Together we walk through the dimming glow,
Hand in hand, our spirits flow.

In this quiet space, we share our dreams,
Building our futures, or so it seems.
Light in the dusk, a promise anew,
In the heart of the night, I find you.

Serendipity's Glow

Fate takes a turn, a gentle surprise,
In unexpected moments, our laughter lies.
Like fireflies dancing in the soft night air,
Serendipity smiles, a gift so rare.

Paths intertwine with a sweet, soft grace,
In the chaos of life, we find our place.
Threads of the cosmos guide us along,
In the chorus of chance, we dance to our song.

Golden moments linger, tender and bright,
We embrace the magic that feels so right.
Each twist and turn brings us delight,
In serendipity's glow, we find our light.

Every glance shared, a spark ignites,
In the heart of the night, our future excites.
Together we wander, hand in hand,
In serendipity's glow, we understand.

Heartbeats of Happiness

In the rhythm of joy, our hearts unite,
Each pulse a promise, vibrant and bright.
Laughter resounds like a sweet summer song,
In moments we cherish, we truly belong.

Sunshine spills over the morning dew,
Awakening dreams that feel like new.
Every heartbeat whispers, 'You are enough,'
In the embrace of love, life's a dance, not rough.

Together we wander through fields of gold,
In stories of joy, our lives unfold.
Collecting heartbeats, moments divine,
In the garden of happiness, our souls entwine.

As twilight descends, we hold on tight,
In the warmth of our hearts, everything feels right.
Echoes of laughter linger near,
In the symphony of life, we conquer fear.

Flickers of Delight

In the garden, light takes flight,
Petals dance in golden sight,
Softly whispering the breeze,
Joyful hearts are sure to seize.

Laughter echoes through the day,
In shadows where children play,
Moments woven, pure and bright,
Each a spark, a flickered light.

Evening falls with warmest glow,
Painting skies in vibrant flow,
Stars prepare to shine and wink,
In this bliss, we're free to think.

Time stands still, pure wonders grow,
In the dance of twilight's show,
Together, here, we share delight,
Flickers fading into night.

Radiance in Dusk

The sun bows down to kiss the sea,
Colors merge in harmony,
Silhouettes against the flame,
Every heart ignites a name.

Whispers soft of evening's grace,
Each shadow finds its rightful place,
In the calm, a vibrant hush,
Nature pauses, feels the rush.

Moments held like fragile glass,
As the world begins to pass,
Glowing embers, warm embrace,
In the dusk, we find our space.

Starlit dreams begin to wake,
In this quiet, we partake,
Together we will find our way,
Radiance in the end of day.

Glimmers of Euphoria

In the meadow, laughter sings,
Far and wide, the joy it brings,
Colors bursting, hearts in bloom,
Life ignites, dispels the gloom.

Morning dew on blades of green,
Every sparkle, pure and keen,
Hopeful visions chase the light,
Glimmers dance to morning's flight.

Chasing dreams that take the air,
Moments wrapped in love and care,
Euphoria whispers through the day,
As the shadows fade away.

Sunset paints the sky with grace,
Leaving warmth in its embrace,
Together hearts forever strive,
In the glow, we feel alive.

Whispers of Elation

In the stillness, moments pause,
Each breath cherished without cause,
Nature hums a gentle tune,
Whispers echo, night and noon.

Stars above like diamonds glow,
Secrets in their shimmer show,
Embraced within a tranquil night,
Elation blooms in pure delight.

Dreams arise like soft, sweet sighs,
Lifted high through velvet skies,
With each heartbeat, joy unfolds,
Stories deep, forever told.

In the warmth of twilight grace,
Every worry finds its place,
Together, we will find our way,
In whispers of elation, stay.

Aura of Blissfulness

In the morning glow, light softly shines,
Whispers of joy dance through the pines.
A heart so free, it learns to soar,
Through waves of peace, forevermore.

With every breath, the world unfolds,
In hues of beauty, stories told.
Serenity wrapped in a gentle hug,
Wrapped in dreams, a warm snug.

Nature's grace flows in gentle streams,
Cascading laughter, unraveling dreams.
A moment cherished, a timeless bliss,
In the soft embrace, we find our kiss.

Under the skies where the colors play,
The soul awakens to another day.
Embracing light with open heart,
An aura of joy, a true work of art.

In a world where hope reigns supreme,
We find our purpose in every beam.
Together we rise, together we sing,
In the aura of bliss, our spirits take wing.

Glowing Tributes

Stars above twinkle with grace,
Each one a memory, a warm embrace.
Illuminating paths, guiding light,
In the whispers of the endless night.

To those who've gone, we raise a cheer,
A tribute glowing, forever near.
Their laughter echoes in the breeze,
A symphony of love that always frees.

With every flicker, a story's told,
Hearts intertwined, forever bold.
In the silence, a gentle call,
In glowing warmth, we honor all.

The candle's dance speaks of the past,
In its soft light, our bonds hold fast.
Each glowing tribute, a heartfelt prayer,
In the fabric of time, always there.

Beneath the moon, shadows play,
In the light, we find our way.
Together we shine, together we'll stand,
In glowing tributes, hand in hand.

Tender Sparks

In quiet moments, love ignites,
Tiny embers glow through starry nights.
Whispers shared in a soft embrace,
Tender sparks light up the space.

When laughter bubbles and hearts align,
A simple glance, the stars entwine.
With each heartbeat, a flame doth grow,
Tender magic in the afterglow.

Beneath the canvas of the twilight sky,
Dreams unfurl, wings learn to fly.
Each spark a promise, a story new,
In tender moments, love shines through.

An evening breeze carries sweet scents,
Of cherished memories, unwavering intents.
In the tapestry woven, our souls embark,
Guided forever by tender sparks.

As shadows dance and daylight fades,
We walk together through life's parades.
Intertwined hearts, forever we'll mark,
The light of our love, those tender sparks.

Flashes of Optimism

In the dawn of day, hope breaks through,
A world awaits, fresh and new.
With every heartbeat, dreams arise,
Flashes of light paint the skies.

Through clouds of doubt, the sun will shine,
A beacon bright, a hopeful line.
In waves of courage, we find our way,
Flashes of optimism guide our stay.

Each step forward ignites a flame,
A journey begun, we'll never be the same.
With vision clear, we'll chase our fate,
In flashes of insight, we celebrate.

The winds of change breathe life anew,
In hearts aflame, we build, we strew.
With kindness shared and spirits bold,
Flashes of optimism, a sight to behold.

Together we rise, unbound and free,
In every heartbeat, a symphony.
With laughter echoing, our spirits climb,
In flashes of hope, our dreams align.

Nightfire Reflections

The embers glimmer in the dark,
Whispers of dreams ignite a spark.
Moonlit shadows dance so high,
In silence, deep, the night draws nigh.

Stars above like distant friends,
Woven tales that never ends.
Through the veil of misty skies,
Hope is found in hidden sighs.

Beneath the glow of fading light,
Fears dissolve, take flight from sight.
Each flicker tells a secret story,
In the night, we find our glory.

Reflections cast in fire's embrace,
Time stands still in this sacred space.
Hearts entwined in warmth and grace,
In nightfire's glow, we find our place.

Hybrid Heat of Happiness

In the mix of sun and shade,
Laughter blooms, its joy displayed.
Flowers rise, a vibrant hues,
In the warmth, the heart renews.

Golden rays kiss the earth,
Every moment, a chance for mirth.
Together we spin, a joyful dance,
In hybrid heat, we take a chance.

Beneath the branches, shadows play,
Whispers of love in bright array.
Joyful echoes fill the air,
In this bliss, we shed our care.

A blend of colors and sweet delight,
Filling souls with purest light.
As we bask in laughter's tide,
In hybrid heat, our hearts abide.

Mirage of Luminous Days

A flicker on the distant shore,
Promises made to seek and soar.
Waves of light caress the land,
Visions painted, soft and grand.

In the distance, hope may gleam,
A shimmering, elusive dream.
Hands stretched out to touch the sky,
In mirage's dance, we learn to fly.

Moments fleeting, like sand through time,
Echoes of laughter, a distant chime.
Every heartbeat a fleeting play,
In luminous days, we find our way.

Reality bends in sunlit haze,
Life's a canvas, endless maze.
Chasing shadows that gleam and sway,
In a mirage of vibrant days.

Celestial Radiance

Stars whisper secrets from afar,
Guiding boats where dreams are.
Each twinkle carries tales untold,
In the cosmos, mysteries unfold.

Moonlight bathes the tranquil sea,
A touch of grace, soft and free.
Waves that dance in silver streams,
In celestial radiance, we weave our dreams.

Galaxies swirl in a cosmic flight,
Painting darkness with bursts of light.
Infinite wonders, we gaze in awe,
Held by nature's timeless law.

Embrace the night, let visions soar,
In the quiet, hear life's roar.
With every glance at skies so wide,
We find our place, our hearts abide.

Radiant Whispers

In the quiet of the dawn,
Soft melodies take flight,
Gentle breezes carry songs,
Whispers of pure light.

Colors dance on morning dew,
Nature's brushstrokes play,
Each leaf shimmers with the glow,
Of the breaking day.

Voices of the earth align,
In harmony they sing,
Threads of warmth entwined with hope,
Endless love they bring.

Under skies of pastel hues,
Dreams begin to soar,
Radiant whispers fill the air,
Calling us for more.

Through the stillness, heartbeats rise,
In a symphony we find,
Every secret moment shared,
With the world unlined.

Sparks in the Darkness

In shadows deep, a flicker glows,
A dance of light appears,
Through the veil of endless night,
Whispers drown our fears.

Stars ignite the velvet sky,
Each twinkle tells a tale,
Of dreams that blossom, hearts set free,
On hope's enchanting trail.

With every spark that dares to shine,
A promise starts to grow,
In the darkness, embers rise,
Creating stars below.

Moments lost in time's embrace,
Will always find their way,
For every shadow knows the light,
Will never fade away.

So let your heart spark brightly now,
And light the paths we roam,
In the depths, we'll always find,
A place we call our home.

Sunkissed Glow

When morning breaks with golden rays,
And paints the world anew,
Each petal drinks the sunlight's kiss,
A vibrant, warm debut.

Fields of amber, waves of gold,
Bathe in warmth and cheer,
Nature smiles with open arms,
As we draw ever near.

Moments wrapped in warm embrace,
Time feels slow and bright,
Sunkissed souls in symphony,
Dancing in pure light.

Let laughter ring through open fields,
Pure joy will surely flow,
When hearts align with nature's grace,
In that sunkissed glow.

As shadows stretch to bid goodbye,
We hold the light so tight,
In memories forged on sunlit paths,
We chase away the night.

Illuminated Moments

In a flash, the world ignites,
With colors swirling bright,
Every second holds a spark,
A kiss from fleeting light.

Through laughter shared and tears that fall,
Life paints a timeless scene,
In illuminated moments,
We find what might have been.

Captured whispers in the dark,
Fleeting, yet profound,
Each heartbeat holds an echo,
In the silence all around.

Hold these moments close and dear,
Like treasures in your heart,
For in each flicker of delight,
New journeys will impart.

A tapestry of light and love,
We weave with every breath,
In illuminated moments,
We find our fullest depth.

Luminous Echoes

In the hush of twilight's breath,
Whispers dance on golden beams.
Stars awaken from their rest,
Casting dreams in silver streams.

Moonlight drapes the silent sea,
Shimmering waves, a soft caress.
Each ripple holds a melody,
In this night, the heart finds rest.

Secrets linger in the air,
Voices of the past ignite.
In the shadows, stories share,
Echoes woven through the night.

Embers glow in gentle hands,
Guiding us to paths unknown.
Each moment like shifting sands,
In their warmth, we are not alone.

So let the echoes softly lead,
Through the dark, we'll share our song.
In the luminous, we take heed,
For together, we belong.

Mosaic of Merriment

Colors splash upon the page,
Laughter blooms in vibrant hues.
Every moment, a new stage,
Where joy resides, each spirit renews.

Candles flicker, shadows play,
Brightening corners, love's embrace.
Each small gesture finds a way,
To weave together heart and space.

In the laughter, we unite,
Crafting memories, bright and clear.
With each smile, we take flight,
Creating bonds that draw us near.

Through the dance, we find our song,
Steps that twirl and spin with glee.
In this mosaic, we belong,
A tapestry of harmony.

So let us weave this joyful thread,
With every heartbeat, every cheer.
In this merriment, we're led,
Bringing light to those held dear.

Kindled Whimsy

Bubbles rise in twilight air,
Softly bursting, laughter spry.
In each gleam, a tender care,
Twirling dreams that float and fly.

Wishes dance on playful winds,
Sailing hearts to far-off lands.
With a spark, an adventure begins,
Playing out as fate commands.

Glimmers in the afternoon,
Sunlight twinkling through the trees.
In every note, a happy tune,
Carried forth by gentle breeze.

Chasing shadows, we will roam,
Finding treasures in the night.
In our hearts, we make a home,
Guided by the stars so bright.

Kindled whimsy in our grasp,
Moments woven, wild and free.
In our laughter, we'll unclasp,
A world of joy, eternally.

Daydreams in Glow

Golden rays filter down low,
Bathing fields in gentle light.
In the warmth, our spirits flow,
Chasing hopes that take to flight.

Dancing petals kiss the ground,
Whispering secrets in the breeze.
In this magic, love is found,
Every heartbeat, soft as leaves.

Clouds drift lazily up high,
Painting stories in the sky.
With a glance, we wave goodbye,
To the mundane that passes by.

In our hearts, the dreams will swell,
Boundless visions crafted slow.
Each day a tale, a wondrous spell,
As we wander through the glow.

So let's embrace each fleeting hour,
With every heartbeat, shape our way.
In daydreams, we hold the power,
To cherish life, a bright ballet.

Softly Burning Dreams

In whispers of the night, we roam,
Where shadows dance, and dreams find home.
A flicker of hope within our sight,
Softly burning, a gentle light.

Each heartbeat whispers tales untold,
Of wishes cast and secrets bold.
The stars, they twinkle, guiding the way,
To softly burning dreams we sway.

With every breath, a wish ignites,
In the stillness, our hearts unite.
Like embers glowing, warm and bright,
Softly burning through the night.

The moon's embrace cradles our fears,
As we weave memories through the years.
In this magic, we find our stream,
Floating softly on burning dreams.

So let us wander in twilight's gleam,
Exploring the wonders of each beam.
With hearts ablaze, together we'll stay,
Softly burning dreams lead our way.

Cascade of Cheer

A river of laughter flows so bright,
Sparkling joy in the morning light.
Each drop a smile, a joyful sound,
A cascade of cheer all around.

With every ripple, our spirits rise,
Underneath the endless skies.
We join the dance, hand in hand,
In this vibrant, magical land.

The flowers bloom, painting the green,
With colors of happiness, pure and clean.
As nature sings, hearts intertwine,
In the cascade where our joy will shine.

Moments of laughter, sweet and clear,
Echo through the hearts we hold dear.
Together, we weave a joyful song,
In this cascade, we all belong.

So let the currents carry us high,
With every wave, we learn to fly.
A waterfall of cheer, our hearts steer,
Toward the horizon, forever near.

Firefly Serenade

In twilight's embrace, the fireflies play,
Dancing softly in the fading day.
Their glow ignites the night's sweet tune,
A serenade beneath the moon.

Twinkling stars in the darkened skies,
Whisper secrets where magic lies.
In a flicker, we lose our cares,
As fireflies weave through the evening air.

Each spark a note in the night's refrain,
Calling us to join their joyful train.
With gentle wings, they softly glide,
In this serenade, we take pride.

As shadows linger, the world grows still,
In the heartbeat of dusk, we feel the thrill.
Embraced by light, our spirits soar,
In the firefly serenade, we explore.

With every flicker, a dream takes flight,
We dance together in soft moonlight.
In this ballet of stars and trees,
The firefly serenade, a sweet breeze.

Dancing Lights of Affection

In the quiet glow of evening's grace,
We find our hearts in a warm embrace.
With every laugh, the shadows play,
Dancing lights of affection sway.

Golden hues paint the darkened skies,
Reflecting love in each other's eyes.
Through whispers of night, our dreams take flight,
In this dance of joy, everything feels right.

Kindred spirits beneath the stars,
We chase the night, forgetting scars.
The gentle rhythm of love's sweet song,
Guides our feet as we move along.

In twinkling lights, our wishes bloom,
Filling the air with a sweet perfume.
As the world around starts to fade,
We hold onto this love we've made.

With every beat, our hearts align,
In this celebration, pure and divine.
Together forever, we brightly say,
Dancing lights of affection lead our way.

Echoes of Laughter

In the park, children play,
With laughter that floats away,
Chasing dreams under the sun,
Moments shared, hearts on the run.

Whispers of joy fill the air,
A melody light and rare,
With every giggle and cheer,
The world feels bright and clear.

Footsteps dance on soft grass,
In time with the moments that pass,
Each echo a story untold,
Memories treasured like gold.

Under the shade, stories unfold,
Of friendship and love, bold,
Together we weave, side by side,
In laughter, our spirits abide.

As shadows grow long at dusk,
Filling the heart with trust,
We take with us what we found,
Echoes of laughter, profound.

Sparks of Hope

In the dark where shadows lie,
A flicker appears in the sky,
Holding dreams full of grace,
Whispers of light in this place.

Through the night, a candle glows,
Its warmth in the heart still flows,
Guiding the lost through despair,
With every glimmer, hope is there.

Each spark a promise to share,
In the silence, hear the prayer,
Together we'll rise from the fall,
With courage, we'll stand tall.

As dawn breaks, colors ignite,
Filling the world with pure light,
Every moment fiercely bright,
Sparks of hope take flight.

In the journey, we'll find our way,
Embracing each new day,
With every heartbeat, we cope,
In the shadows, we find hope.

Flames of Serenity

In the stillness of the night,
A flickering flame, soft and bright,
Whispers of peace wrap around,
In its glow, calmness is found.

Embers dance with graceful cheer,
Chasing away every fear,
The warmth hugs like a soft breeze,
In the moment, we find ease.

Moments held in quiet grace,
Time slows down in this place,
Each heartbeat a soothing song,
With solace that can't be wrong.

As shadows retreat and fade,
In serenity, dreams are made,
The heart learns to embrace,
Flames of peace in life's race.

With ashen trails of the past,
We find love that will last,
In the warmth of each other's eyes,
Serenity, where truth lies.

A Dance of Gleeful Glimmers

Under stars, the world will sway,
In a dance that lights the way,
Glimmers of joy lead us through,
In the night, dreams are new.

Every twirl, a story spun,
Guiding hearts, two become one,
Laughter echoes, soft and sweet,
In this rhythm, we feel complete.

With every beat, the cosmos spins,
Each step a chance, a dance begins,
Gleeful shines spark in the dark,
Igniting hopes, a tiny spark.

As moonlight spills on the ground,
Where love and joy can be found,
A fleeting moment in time,
Where every heartbeat feels like rhyme.

Together we weave our night,
With glimmers of pure delight,
In this dance, we will glide,
Gleeful spirits open wide.

Flickers of Delight

In the garden where laughter blooms,
Joy dances lightly, dispelling glooms.
Colors vivid in the morning light,
Hearts awaken, embracing the bright.

Sparrows chirp, a sweet serenade,
Time slows down, in this fair parade.
Each moment savored, a gentle flight,
Life's simple pleasures, pure delight.

The sun dips low, painting the sky,
As fireflies flicker, they start to fly.
A soft whisper, an echoing night,
In every pulse, there's pure delight.

Children play under stars that gleam,
In this canvas, we weave a dream.
Hand in hand, we'll chase the night,
In the magic of moment, pure delight.

With every breath, our spirits rise,
Caught in the web of starlit ties.
A fleeting glance, a shared insight,
Forever captured, moments of delight.

Whispers of Warmth

Amidst the chill of winter's breath,
We gather close, defying death.
Fires crackle, casting golden light,
In the warmth, we find our might.

Soft embraces, comfort shared,
In every touch, love's essence dared.
With gentle words, we reunite,
In the whispers that spark the night.

Snowflakes twirl, a silent glide,
Outside the storm, we bide our tide.
With cocoa cups held close and tight,
In each other's hearts, warmth ignites.

Tales of old around the flame,
Every voice lifts, none the same.
In memories sewn, we unite,
With whispers echoing, warmth shines bright.

As daylight breaks, the frost will flee,
In this haven, we feel so free.
Together we'll face the morning light,
With every heartbeat, whispers of warmth.

Glimmers of Bliss

In twilight's glow, we find our peace,
Where gentle sighs and troubles cease.
The horizon bathes in a soft kiss,
In this space, we find our bliss.

Petals unfurl, a fragrant dream,
Rivers of laughter, a brightened stream.
With every glance, your eyes hold this,
A magic moment, filled with bliss.

Stars awaken, sprinkling the night,
Each twinkle a promise, a guiding light.
Hand in hand, we chase the mist,
In our souls, we harbor bliss.

Time flows gently, as shadows play,
Together we'll wander, come what may.
In the silent whispers, hearts enlist,
Every moment wraps us in bliss.

As dawn approaches, dreams take flight,
In your embrace, the world feels right.
With every heartbeat, love's sweet kiss,
In this journey, we find our bliss.

Radiance in the Shadows

In the depths where dark whispers hum,
A light flickers, a distant drum.
Through the shadows, hope starts to rise,
With every heartbeat, a new surprise.

Moments linger, like secrets shared,
In the silence, our hearts laid bare.
Even in darkness, find the ties,
That weave radiance, hidden in lies.

Stars above twinkle like dreams,
Illuminating paths, or so it seems.
In the night's embrace, we realize,
There's radiance even when love sighs.

With every tear, let the past flow,
As dawn's touch brings a gentle glow.
The shadows flee, with morning cries,
In the light, we find our wise.

Together we stand, come what may,
In darkness or light, we'll find our way.
With courage born from love's replies,
We'll discover radiance in the shadows.

Chasing the Afterglow

In twilight's warm embrace, we roam,
Fingers tracing dreams, far from home.
Stars awaken, bright and bold,
In whispers of stories yet untold.

With every breath, the night unfolds,
A tapestry woven with threads of gold.
The sky blushes as day takes flight,
While shadows dance, lost in the night.

Hearts racing with the fading light,
Chasing echoes of sweet delight.
A symphony sung by the evening breeze,
We chase the afterglow with ease.

In laughter and sighs, our spirits soar,
Each moment cherished, we long for more.
Underneath the indigo sky,
We'll continue to reach, and never say goodbye.

As dawn approaches, we dare to dream,
Finding solace in a silver beam.
For in the afterglow, we find our way,
Holding tightly to the close of day.

Echoes of Radiance

In the silence of twilight's song,
Radiance echoes, sweet and strong.
Memories shimmer in fading light,
Drawing us closer, banishing fright.

With whispers carried on gentle winds,
A tale of love that never ends.
Bright constellations lead the way,
Guiding our hearts where dreams sway.

In the embrace of night, we find,
Echoes of laughter, hearts entwined.
Each flicker of starlight, a gentle kiss,
A reminder of moments we dare not miss.

As shadows stretch and time stands still,
We dance together, lost in will.
Beneath the moon's radiant glow,
We are the echoes, forever aglow.

With every heartbeat, the world fades,
In echoes of radiance, love cascades.
Forever bound by the starry sky,
In each other's arms, we learn to fly.

Flickering Happiness

In the stillness of the morning light,
Flickering shadows dance in delight.
Joy hangs softly like dew on grass,
Each moment fleeting, yet sure to last.

With laughter rising like a soft breeze,
We find happiness among the trees.
Sunshine beams through branches wide,
A gentle reminder, never to hide.

In the rustling leaves, life whispers sweet,
Flickering happiness beneath our feet.
Every glance, a spark of glee,
In simple things, we find the key.

As the day folds into amber glow,
We gather memories, letting them flow.
The heart's warmth never fades away,
In flickering moments, we choose to stay.

With every heartbeat, love's embrace,
Flickering happiness finds its place.
Forever cherished, forever known,
In our hearts, we've made a home.

Scent of Sweet Nostalgia

In the air, a fragrant breeze,
Whispers of past, carried with ease.
Like blooms unfolding in the sun,
The scent of nostalgia has begun.

Memories wrapped in petals bright,
Take me back to warm delight.
With every breath, the past awakes,
In each sweet moment, our heart breaks.

Through winding paths of time we tread,
Chasing echoes of things once said.
In laughter and tears, we find our way,
Nostalgia's embrace here to stay.

Beneath the twilight, we stand in awe,
Capturing fleeting moments we saw.
The scent of sweet nostalgia sings,
A melody of warmth that forever clings.

So let us cherish what once was ours,
Gathering memories like shooting stars.
In the gentle perfume of yesteryears,
We find our solace, we find our tears.

Glint of Gaiety

In the morning light, a smile plays,
Joy dances in the sun's warm rays.
Laughter spills like a crystal stream,
Life weaves magic, akin to a dream.

Children's voices ring through the air,
Colors bright, with love to spare.
Every moment, a treasure to hold,
Stories of joy, waiting to be told.

On the winds, whispers of delight,
Stars twinkle softly, embracing the night.
Hearts entwined in moments so sweet,
Together they make this life complete.

Clouds drift gently, the world feels right,
With every heartbeat, pure delight.
Nature sings in a vibrant tune,
Beneath a sky, a radiant moon.

In laughter's echo, we find our way,
Chasing shadows that dance and sway.
With each glint, a promise unfolds,
A tapestry woven, where happiness molds.

Thresholds of Hope

On the edge of dawn, new dreams arise,
A canvas painted with open skies.
Whispers of courage, bold and bright,
Guiding us forward, into the light.

Each step taken is a story new,
With paths unknown, yet so true.
In the silence, we find our voice,
In every heartbeat, we make our choice.

Mountains may rise, and rivers may bend,
But hope is a journey that won't end.
Through shadows and doubts, we push ahead,
Nurturing visions that dreams have bred.

The stars above us shine steadfast,
Reminding us that trials won't last.
With open hearts, we break through the gloom,
Embracing horizons where wild flowers bloom.

Thresholds await, with doors ajar,
Inviting us boldly to travel far.
With each step forward, faith leads the way,
To brighter tomorrows, come what may.

Radiant Journeys

On winding roads where shadows play,
Adventures beckon, leading the way.
Every sunrise paints a new scene,
Transforming the ordinary to serene.

With every heartbeat, stories unfold,
Moments captured, memories hold.
Through fields of gold and skies so blue,
Life's radiant journeys await to pursue.

Beneath the stars, our dreams ignite,
Exploring the vastness of the night.
Winds of change sweep past our feet,
Guiding us gently on paths so sweet.

In the laughter we share, bonds grow strong,
In harmony's rhythm, we find where we belong.
Each step we take, a dance of delight,
As we weave through the fabric of night.

Carried by hope, like a flowing stream,
We chase the dawn, we dare to dream.
Radiant journeys, forever we seek,
In the light of our spirits, we find our peak.

Fragments of Bliss

In fleeting moments, joys combine,
A tapestry woven, soft and fine.
Fragments of bliss, stitched with care,
Whispers of love linger in the air.

The taste of sunshine on a warm breeze,
Petals of flowers dance with ease.
In the stillness, peace finds its place,
Every heartbeat adorned with grace.

With laughter shared around the fire,
Stories unfold, hearts inspired.
Candles flicker, shadows play near,
In comforting spaces, we hold them dear.

Through simple pleasures, treasures arise,
In each soft moment, a sweet surprise.
Hidden in corners, joy blooms free,
Fragments of bliss, like drops in the sea.

In the echoes of laughter, life's sweet kiss,
We embrace these fragments, savoring bliss.
Together we gather, hearts aligned,
In the dance of existence, happiness defined.

The Warmth of Togetherness

In the glow of fading light,
We gather close, hearts ignite.
Whispers soft like summer rain,
In this moment, love remains.

Fingers laced in tender trust,
Together strong, we find our must.
Each laugh a spark, each tear a flow,
In this bond, we brightly grow.

Time stands still, the world outside,
In your arms, I feel the tide.
Breath of peace, a gentle sigh,
Underneath the vast, wide sky.

Every secret shared, a thread,
Woven deep, our lives are led.
Through the storms and sunlit bliss,
In this togetherness, we exist.

A tapestry of moments spun,
In every heartbeat, we are one.
With every look, with every smile,
In your presence, I'll stay awhile.

Fragments of Euphoria

In the quiet of the morn,
Joy dances, dreams are born.
Moments flash like shooting stars,
In the night, we'll raise our bars.

Every laugh, a drop of light,
Purest happiness takes flight.
Chasing echoes through the air,
Fragments of a love we share.

Colors swirl in morning's haze,
Painting life in vibrant ways.
Each heartbeat sings a tender song,
In this bliss, we both belong.

Fleeting seconds, crystal clear,
Embracing joy, casting fear.
Every glance, electric spark,
In this dance, ignite the dark.

Breathe in deep, let worries flee,
Moments rise like waves at sea.
With you, love, I am alive,
In this euphoria, we thrive.

Chasing the Light

Through the shadows, hope will gleam,
We wander paths where visions dream.
Every step, a fleeting chance,
In the dawn, our spirits dance.

With each sunrise comes our quest,
To grasp the light, to be our best.
Holding hands, we cross the line,
Together, hearts and dreams entwine.

The horizon calls, so bright, so clear,
As we chase away all fear.
In the laughter, in the play,
We find our joy, we find our way.

Clouds may gather, storms may rage,
Yet love's warmth turns every page.
With you beside me, I can climb,
Chasing the light, one day at a time.

Whispers of the stars at night,
Guide our hearts towards the light.
In our journey, hand in hand,
We'll write our dreams in golden sand.

The Joyful Flame

In the heart, there burns a fire,
Whispers soft of deep desire.
Flickering bright, it lights our way,
In the night, our spirits play.

With every laugh, the embers glow,
In this warmth, we'll always know.
Together in this joyful dance,
Life ignites with every chance.

Through the rain and through the storm,
Our love creates a shelter warm.
With each challenge, we find grace,
In this flame, we find our place.

And in the quiet, after all,
We feel the rhythm, hear the call.
Holding tight, we stoke the flame,
In our hearts, it stays the same.

Forever bright, eternally,
The joyful flame will always be.
Through every trial, through every cheer,
In this love, we have no fear.

www.ingramcontent.com/pod-product-compliance
Ingram Content Group UK Ltd.
Pitfield, Milton Keynes, MK11 3LW, UK
UKHW021642200125
4187UKWH00003B/240